DOG WORKS

The Meaning and Magic of Canine Constructions

By Vicki Mathison

· · · · · · · · · · · · · · · · ·

Photographs by

Tim Dodgshun

Trudy Nicholson

TEN SPEED PRESS

Berkeley / Toronto

DOG WORKS

The Meaning and Magic of Canine Constructions

TEN SPEED PRESS
P.O. Box 7123
Berkeley, California 94707
www.tenspeed.com

Distributed in Australia by Simon and Schuster Australia, in Canada by Ten Speed Press Canada, in New Zealand by Southern Publishers Group, in South Africa by Real Books, in Southeast Asia by Berkeley Books, and in the United Kingdom and Europe by Airlift Book Company.

The moral rights of Vicki Mathison (as author),
Tim Dodgshun and Trudy Nicholson (as photographers)
and Helene Saville (as illustrator) to be identified as creators
of this work has been asserted by them in accordance
with the Copyright, Designs, and Patents Act, 1988.

Compiled by Origination Press
487 Karaka Bay Rd., Wellington 3
New Zealand

Editorial director: Melissa da Souza.
Originated, devised, and designed by Melissa da Souza
and Vicki Mathison.

Library of Congress Cataloging-in-Publication Data is
on file with the publisher.

ISBN: 1–58008–244–0

First USA printing, 2000

Printed and bound in China

1 2 3 4 5—04 03 02 01 00

Dedicated to the memory of Minka and Titch.

"Fly softly sweet Minks—my forever dog."

"Sun, saltwater, sticks & sand—
Fish & chips—your leash in my hand."
To Titch—Love, Bella

TABLE OF CONTENTS

Introduction   8

A Scientist's View   10

A Spiritual Link   12

TWENTY-FIVE CANINE ARTISTS

TOWSER — AN IRISH WOLFHOUND   14

HARRY — A JACK RUSSELL TERRIER   18

KATYA — A POODLE-SPANIEL MIX   20

JESSIE — A PUREBRED BOXER   24

JEMIMA — A CORGI-SHELTIE MIX   30

SHADOW — A BLACK LABRADOR   34

DASH — A BORDER COLLIE   38

SHYLO — A PUREBRED BEAGLE   42

MINKA — A STANDARD POODLE   44

EMILY — A STAFFORDSHIRE BULL TERRIER   48

FLOSSIE — A WHEATEN TERRIER   52

BUCK — A PUREBRED DALMATIAN   56

LUKE — AN ALASKAN MALAMUTE   58

TITCH — A ROTTWEILER-LABRADOR MIX   64

KAYSEE — A CAIRN TERRIER   68

ABBIE — A SHETLAND SHEEPDOG   72

ZETA — AN AUSTRALIAN KELPIE   74

TEDDY — A GOLDEN RETRIEVER   78

RENEGADE — A GERMAN SHEPHERD   82

OCHRE — A HUNGARIAN VIZSLA   84

JEDA AND BLAKEY — BELGIAN BARGE DOGS   88

MCCOY AND THE GROUP   92

What Will My Dog Do?   94

Acknowledgements   96

Select Bibliography   96

INTRODUCTION

A dog did that."

The concept of *Dog Works* was born during a sandstorm on a beach when I stumbled upon seven lined-up holes that had an intriguing symmetry. The setting sun cast deep shadows both in the holes and to their sides, and the racing sand had smoothed their rims to gentle undulations, giving the appearance of soft sand nests.

The holes were obviously not a natural occurrence. My assumption was that here was the work of an artist, modified by the sculpting effect of the sandstorm.

"A dog did that," came the voice of a strolling passerby. "I saw it. It was digging in that last hole."

Ever skeptical, I assumed that the dog had discovered the holes and had been observed in the process of investigating, as dogs do.

Further up the beach I met a couple with a Golden Retriever and broached the subject of the sculpted sand nests. They had also seen the

same dog digging at that site—but there were only two holes at the time. A shadow of doubt crept over my original supposition and I decided to track down the dog and her owner.

The alleged canine sculptor was a small Corgi-Sheltie mix named Jemima. Her owner was somewhat surprised at the interest engendered by Jemima's behavior, as hole-digging was a regular activity for this dog. However, he did concede that the juxtaposition of the holes and their relative symmetry might be unusual. Apparently Jemima had at first dug holes in random configurations, but over time began to align them. He also mentioned that after completing her series of holes, the dog would nestle into the hollow of the last one and remain inert for up to ten minutes. "Almost as though she had built herself a nest."

I was convinced that the dog's performance was indeed unusual—if not unique—but the niggling question remained: if this dog builds sand nests, what might other dogs build, and above all, *why?*

For some time I had been questioning the narrow range of ways of communicating ascribed to dogs by biologists and animal behaviorists. Thought transference and recognition of symbols—e.g., car keys mean a potential walk—were about as far as I had hypothesized. After meeting Jemima and seeing her work I decided to investigate further. A small article I placed in animal publications and newsletters and on the Internet together with a request for information from anyone knowing of dogs who exhibited unusual artistic behavior instigated a tide of letters and phone calls.

I received communication from a surprising 155 owners or observers, 40 percent of whom I disregarded, as their stories were either unverifiable or included unbelievable, unremarkable, or bizarre behaviors often involving other animals such as goats, cats, horses, and even a painting otter. This initial screening left ninety-three to investigate further.

My interest in documenting the selected works of dogs was increased by a chance meeting with an animal psychologist who put me in touch with Penelope Winter and Dr. Raymond Blake, two animal experts from opposing camps who both work outside the accepted parameters of dog behavior. Armed with photographers and these two experts we embarked on a project that has had the effect of challenging my beliefs about the capabilities of dogs and the reasons behind their behavior.

—*Vicki Mathison*

A Scientist's View

Every human child must learn the universe afresh. Every stockdog pup carries the universe within him. Humans have externalized their wisdom—stored it in museums, libraries, the expertise of the learned. Dog wisdom is inside the blood and bones."

—*Donald McCaig, writer.*

Genetic inheritance denotes not only physical features, temperament, and a predisposition for certain diseases and abnormalities but also behavioral tendencies and expertise in specific areas. This is particularly apparent in dogs bred for specific functions, e.g., sheepdogs, retrievers, guard dogs, sight hounds, scent hounds, and diggers. Regardless of whether or not a particular dog has ever been used in its designated capacity, he will have the genetic imprint for that behavior. A herding puppy will begin to show herding behavior from a very young age. A poodle will exhibit retrieving behavior in spite of the fact that poodles have not been used as bird dogs for decades.

Beyond the universal acceptance of genetic inheritance is the work of Dr. Raymond Blake and his Institute of Canine Cultural Heritage. The Institute was established by Dr. Blake and colleagues in 1989 to study causal factors of dog behavior that appeared to lie outside of the parameters of basic genetic shaping yet seemingly retained links to the historic background specific to a breed or to an individual dog.

"The initial motivation to instigate this study was Fritz, a small terrier-mix from Amsterdam who was an inveterate and incurable herder of golf balls. On investigation of his lineage we discovered that his only connection to herders was six generations back and even then the link was tenuous. The possible far-reaching implications of Fritz's apparent genetic memory was the germ of an idea from which the Institute was born."

Blake is a biologist with vitalist leanings—that is, he believes that living matter possesses some extra magic ingredient, a vital force or essence that cannot easily be reduced to mechanical components. His work with the Institute of Canine Cultural Heritage has led him to support the words of Lyall Watson: "DNA doesn't necessarily have the last word."

In *The Selfish Gene* in 1976, Richard Dawkins coined the term *meme* to depict a unit of cultural transmission, a kind of nonphysical gene or abstract DNA. Blake believes that memes or something similar operate in the structure of the subconscious minds of the canine subjects he works with. An idea or behavior not necessarily genetic can be passed through time and generations, resulting in seemingly inexplicable animal actions or responses.

"It's almost as though the animal has a box of inherited transparencies of past experiences. Given a particular trigger, a slide will project forward from the subconscious to the present situation. Frequently the memory will be purely visual, but at times a psychological component will be apparent."

He describes these events as "echoes from the past" or "intergenerational resonances."

A Spiritual Link

Any suggestion that dogs have a spiritual life or the facility of insight, telepathy, and precognition extending beyond the bounds of instinct has been ignored or scornfully dismissed by the scientific community.

There is an insurmountable obstacle to the possibility of biologists and scientists openly accepting the concept of canine telepathy and spirituality: the perceived necessity of using scientific terminology. If animal communication is based on senses we have lost, how can we quantify something we don't understand, can't observe, and don't experience ourselves? However, the spiritual side of animals, dogs in particular, is now being acknowledged by a growing vanguard of influential people within the scientific community.

After experimental tests on canine ESP at Rockland State Hospital in New York, psychiatrist and neurologist Dr. Aristide Esser concludes, "There is no doubt in my mind that some dogs, particularly those with a close relationship with their owners, have highly developed extrasensory perception."

Penelope Winter, an exponent of the interspecies telepathic communication school of thought, shares Esser's conviction.

"Telepathy or thought transference enables humans and animals to share a universal language that is beyond speech. Dogs know this language, and humans have to learn to listen with their hearts and senses. With all our gains in intellect has come a parallel loss: the ability to communicate

directly from mind to mind without the aid or obstacle of the spoken word. Animals have retained this skill, and by learning to connect with them we can increase our own psychic powers."

Winter's interest in the spiritual side of dogs began during her career as a community-health nurse. While visiting elderly people in their homes she began to observe the special relationship between dogs and humans.

"The dogs were obviously of enormous importance and comfort to my elderly patients. As dogs were often my patients' only companions, there was a lot of verbal communication from human to dog. In time, I began to notice signs that a silent connection was happening between some dogs and their owners. For example, a sleeping dog would suddenly leap up and trot toward the kitchen. Seconds later, her owner would ask if I would like a cup of tea. It appeared that through some kind of thought transference, the dog received the idea as it occurred to the owner but before she acted upon it."

The growing conviction that dogs have unique perceptions, intuitive capabilities, and powers of telepathy and precognition inspired Winters to abandon her nursing career and to begin a journey of discovery about the spiritual life of dogs. Her present position on dogs' psychic powers has extended far beyond her initial observations.

"Dogs have a vital connection to the ancient rhythms of the earth, moon, and stars and all planetary changes. They have been known as the guardians of ancient secrets. If we but listen and understand their world, they can act as our healers and teachers."

She now believes not only that messages can be transmitted telepathically between dog and human but also that dogs are also open to communication from the spirit world.

Most wolfhound owners know the legend of the hero hound Gelert. The story begins with a Welsh prince who, upon discovering his infant son missing from his tent and finding his dog covered in blood, kills the dog in a rage. However, Gelert had in fact saved the child from the jaws of a large wolf.

Towser, despite his sleepy appearance, is a hero of similar proportions. While on a long walk with his owners he wandered off the track and stumbled across an abandoned kitten partially hidden by fallen leaves. The kitten was hypothermic, and the wolfhound curled around her and calmly fell asleep. After two hours of frantic calling and searching, Towser's owners discovered him asleep, the kitten tucked beside his thick cream coat. Strangely, the owners had passed within sixty feet of the spot several times during the search but Towser had not responded to their calls.

Towser
An Irish Wolfhound
. . . .

Despite his mammoth proportions, Towser is a classic gentle-giant type. He has a laid-back personality and does not exert himself unless absolutely necessary.

The modern-day Irish Wolfhound is believed by some to be a breed combining the Scottish Deerhound and the Great Dane. Traditionally these dogs were used to hunt elk as well as wolves, although on meeting Towser this is hard to imagine.

Towser is reputed to have a strange relationship with deer antlers. He lives on a deer farm where the antlers are usually attached to their owners' heads, but at shedding time Towser becomes singularly fascinated. He has been observed lurking about the deeryards investigating the fallen antlers before they are gathered up. His owner initially presumed that the dog was interested in the smell of deer blood but realized that the truth was more complex. Towser is not concerned with any lone antler, but when two or more lie in close proximity, he attempts to build a covering structure for each. He uses whatever materials are at hand—sacks, sweaters, sticks—and has even been spotted attempting to hide a set of antlers under a wrecked bicycle frame.

Dr. Raymond Blake, Canine Cultural Heritage Researcher:

"This dog does not regard deer as prey and he shows no predator inclination in their direction. However, he is most definitely responding to ancestral reverberations when confronted with antlers. The fact that one set of antlers does not elicit the same response indicates to me a memory of traditional hunting practices of the Celts. When more than one elk was slain the hunters attempted to camouflage those that could not be immediately carried back to their camp. They achieved this by laying sticks, branches, anything they could find, across the bodies of the deer. On the rare occasions that Towser finds a dead deer on the property he does not attempt to hide it, probably because he has not yet discovered more than one at a time. The distinctive form and smell of a deer antler is imprinted in his shared ancestral history and he is compelled to behave in this unusual manner."

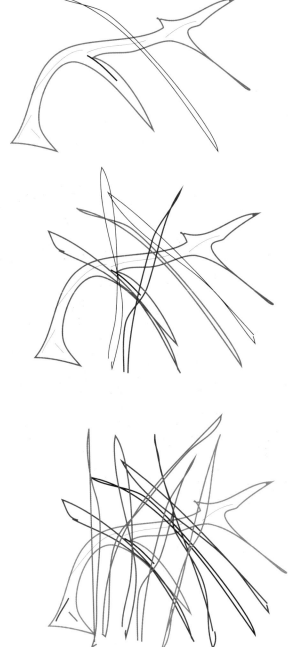

Penelope Winter, Animal Spiritualist and Telepathic Diviner:

"Towser gives the impression of a soul not quite present on the earth plan-et. I had the strong feeling that by witnessing his work we were interrupt-ing his connecting link with another plane. He did not immediately begin his construction but spent some time gazing out to the sea and sky. When he did finally focus on the antlers, he was unstoppable. I feel Towser was involved in a form of channeling or was receiving instructions from an incarnate. His work looks very similar to the old runic symbol of the tree of death, an oathtaking sign used in Celtic times. The word *rune* in Celtic languages means "mystery" or "whispered secret"; perhaps Towser is the receiver of a message from a religious Celtic sect. My spirit guide Fleeing Deer indicates that Towser is being taken over by a disturbed incarnate who wishes to communicate in a physical way.

"Towser looked quite exhausted by the time he had finished his work, a common reaction to being used as a conduit by another being."

Harry takes life very seriously. He lives with two hyperactive Labrador Retrievers and the more boisterously they behave, the more serene he becomes. Like all terriers, Harry loves to dig, but here is where the similarity fades. Most Jack Russells dig with a frightening intensity and disregard for finesse. Harry is meticulous. He begins his projects in an orderly, well-thought-out fashion and quietly perseveres until he is happy with the end result. The Labradors' "digs" have the appearance of a bulldozer out of control whereas Harry's are works of archaeological precision. Spirals became a major trope of inspiration several months ago. Up until then Harry had favored deep holes with tunnels radiating out from the center, rather like a sundial. He began his spiral series in a friend's sandpit and spent an idyllic few hours working from the center in a counterclockwise direction until he hit the wooden rim. Harry always emerges from his digs immaculate and unruffled, wearing a self-satisfied expression.

Harry
A Jack Russell Terrier
. . . .

We were fortunate to catch Harry in a cooperative mood, as he is normally quite camera shy. His owner suggested that we hide behind the sand dunes until he completed the first loop of his spiral; by then he would be so engrossed that our presence would not unsettle him.

Penelope Winter, Animal Spiritualist and Telepathic Diviner:
"Harry's owner told us that Harry's previous digging designs were like a child's early attempts at depicting the sun. He would first dig a substantial hole and then paw out several branches radiating from the center. This makes the meaning of Harry's spirals crystal clear. To the ancient inhabitants of Ireland the spiral symbolized the sun, and a loosely wound counterclockwise form represented the large sun of summer.

"Harry is devoted to the sun. In the height of the summer he basks in its heat while his roommates, the Labradors, seek out shade. I think Harry is so connected to the sun that it is quite natural for him to choose such a design. He is also a Virgo dog. Perseverance and attention to detail are characteristic of beings born under the influence of the sun in Virgo."

Dr. Raymond Blake, Canine Cultural Heritage Researcher:
"Terriers are renowned for digging. They are bred for this very purpose—to excavate and destroy vermin. This dog does not have a vermin-control role but his ancestors certainly did. Harry is programmed to dig. I am not an expert in the habits of rodents, but I have read of the peculiar tunneling designs of the Golden Hamster, first discovered by an English zoologist in Syria. These unique little animals tunneled their breeding holes in a vague spiral configuration, as this was most likely to confuse predators. The zoologist transported the hamsters back to England and apparently all domestic Golden Hamsters are direct descendants of that original family. Harry's grandfather was imported from Britain. According to his breeder, Golden Hamsters were bred on the same property. The connection couldn't be clearer."

Katya began her puppyhood on a chain tied to a rusty barrel. At ten months she changed her address and with it, her lifestyle. Considering that she is such a small dog, Katya's past twelve years have been extraordinarily rich and filled with unusual experiences. Along with being appointed visual arts mascot and staff counselor at her owner's college, she has competed in obedience and agility trials and has made forays into the equivalent of police-dog trials—minus the "man work," of course! While not quite as competent as a Border Collie, Katya has also attempted working sheep. (It was unclear who was actually doing the herding.)

She has no concept of herself as a dog of minuscule proportions. Once she has designated a space as hers it is sacrosanct. Vehicles, horses, and wolfhounds are expected to avoid her personal bubble. Despite near-tragic consequences and a set of hoof prints as a souvenir, Katya sticks to her hypothesis that size is irrelevant. She does not subscribe to Chicken Little's conviction that we are in danger of the sky falling on our heads—quite the reverse.

Katya
A Poodle - Spaniel Mix
· · · · · · · · · · · · · · · ·

Katya is a very small Poodle-Spaniel mix who emanates the presence of a deerhound. Her fascination with wing bones began during the creation of a bone sculpture by her artist owner, Adriane. Katya removed fragile luminous pieces from the construction pile over a period of three days, and they were discovered lined up in groups in various locations around the property.

We took Katya and a pile of assorted objects, including her wing bones, to a local beach. A tiny black dot in the setting sun, she powered back and forth from the pile to the summit of her sand dune hauling large and awkward bones up the steep slope then leaping off the ridge for the repeat journey. She continued for over an hour and seemed loath to leave her completed "sculpture" till the last rays of sun had completely vanished.

Dr. Raymond Blake, Canine Cultural Heritage Researcher:

"My initial interpretation is that the spaniel genes in this dog are dominant over those of the poodle, and what we are seeing here is quite possibly the recreation of passage graves at Los Millares in the North of Spain. These graves were built in Neolithic times and the doorways to the passages always face southwest to allow the midwinter sun to penetrate the burial chamber. Interestingly, skeletons of small dogs have been found in the graves; as they often had ornaments attached to them, they seem to have been kept as pets. Due to their size they were of little or no use for hunting. Analyzing the pagan beliefs held during these times sheds further light on the role of these dogs: they served as companions to the dead on their final journey to the spirit world. Dogs were also an integral part of the building of the passage stones leading to tomb sites. It took many months to maneuver the huge rocks into their final positions, and the dogs were required to lie beside each newly erected stone as part of the ritualistic blessing of its significance to the dead.

"However, I think it unwise to discount Katya's undeniably potent poodle genetic makeup, and I feel that the positioning of the wing bones in a line could have a direct connection to the poodle's retriever history. One of the duties of eighteenth-century gamekeepers was to control birds that were regarded as vermin, mostly birds of prey that endangered the population of pheasants so prized by the aristocracy. To advertise his prowess

and to issue a warning to other birds, a gamekeeper would shoot crows, ravens, and hawks and string up their carcasses along a rope between two poles—a contraption called a gibbet. The retrievers who assisted the gamekeeper in his task would receive their reward after the last bird was in position and so would sit patiently beside the line until they were fed. I think it is quite possible that in this little dog's case, she is creating a symbolic gibbet and continues to do so, as she is undoubtedly rewarded for her 'cleverness' by her owner."

Penelope Winter, Animal Spiritualist and Telepathic Diviner:
"The key to the explanation of this small dog's work is the strong psychic relationship she obviously has with her owner. I can feel their connection on an astral plane and their telepathic communication is very highly developed. When Katya began to work with the bones, her aura, which had been fluctuating between deep rose and blue-green, started to vibrate into a strong blue. This indicates creativity, imagination, and self-expression and depicts the feminine nature. This change in auric color was echoed in that of her owner and I could virtually see the thought transference between them. Even the presence of an audience could not break such a connection, which is quite unusual with human/animal telepathy. We must not overlook that Katya's owner is a sculptor and Katya is her

constant companion in the studio. The similarity in form of her installation on the sand dune to her owner's work is extraordinary; I'm positive that over time they have begun to draw their inspiration from the same source."

Adriane, Katya's Owner:

"I'm convinced that Katya has some form of aesthetic awareness and has deliberately placed the bones in a position to show their strong vertical forms along a soft horizontal base line. Katya has always been attracted to upright, projecting forms. When she plays with toilet-roll tubes, for example, she always props them up on their ends; usually in a line and oriented from northeast to southwest. The students at the art school where Katya spends so much of her time often joke about her role as an art critic. Sometimes she sits as though in assessment mode and contemplates a work with a strange intensity, while she gives only a cursory glance to others, instead wandering off to look for discarded lunchboxes."

Jessie's intended career as a guard dog never really got off the ground, although she comes from a long line of very successful guards and was purchased by her original owner for this purpose. At ten months old she was introduced to guard duty under the supervision of two established dogs. Her boss was alerted that night by frantic barking from the yard and arrived to find the trained dogs snarling ferociously at the wire: Jessie was rapturously licking the hand of a passing teenager. Trained as a pup not to accept food from strangers, even that was forgotten in her enthusiasm for her new friend. Her muzzle was covered with hamburger crumbs and a piece of lettuce hung from one fang like a lace handkerchief. Jessie was given several opportunities to redeem herself, but aggression—real or feigned—just was not part of her repertoire.

Advertised as "Failed guard—Talented Smooch," she found her new home with Carol, who delights in her affectionate nature.

Jessie
A Purebred Boxer
. . . .

Jessie revealed herself as a dog builder during the summer solstice. Her owner, Carol, regularly meditates and is fascinated by the Druid cult's holistic approach to energy balance.

Carol had arranged several large stones in a circle formation as a kind of Druidic site and found that the ritualistic stone ring helped create the ideal atmosphere in which to meditate. Twice a week Carol and Jessie visited the stones and spent long periods sitting quietly in their midst. Jessie, normally exhibiting the boundless energy of a typical boxer, appeared to enjoy the tranquility of these sessions within the circle. In fact, her general character altered considerably once Carol began to include her in the stone-ring meditations. Her boisterous nature changed to something approaching mellow.

Carol, Jessie's Owner:

"One evening Jessie appeared restless and disturbed. She squeezed herself between two of the stones and stared at me with such intensity that it completely put me off my meditation. Every time I called her into the center of the circle, she flattened her ears and looked up at the sky through the gap in the stones. Giving up any further thoughts of a successful meditation session, I gazed at the configuration of rocks and wondered vaguely about building lintels as in the rings of Stonehenge to increase the circle's power. Jessie suddenly projected herself out from behind her stone pillars and rushed off, her stumpy little tail vibrating with excitement. A few minutes later she returned with a piece of driftwood that, to my amazement, she pushed onto the top of two of the stones until it balanced precariously, forming an arch. After a few "clever dog!"s she was on a roll and repeated the exercise on the next two pairs of stones."

Penelope Winter, Animal Spiritualist and Telepathic Diviner:

"Jessie is a particularly sensitive and soulful boxer. She is easily alarmed and very tuned in to her owner's feelings and thoughts.

"The power and psychic energy of stone rings such as Avesbury and

Stonehenge has been accepted for centuries. The circle has been used repeatedly as a symbol of unity, wholeness, the sun, and the earth. Obviously, Jessie is acutely affected by her sessions in her owner's meditation ring, and the telepathic linking between the two is magnified by the energy built up in the circle.

"The interesting thing is that Jessie had sat in the stone circle many times in the past with no obvious need to add to the sculptural nature of the ring. It appears that the difference this time was Carol's thoughts on lintels. This is a lovely example of thought transference, where the owner

visualizes an event and the dog puts it into reality. I do wonder about Jessie's gazing at the sky between the pillars before Carol began musing about the possibility of lintels. Perhaps Jessie did the visualizing first and sent those pictures to Carol? The lintel thoughts were then intensified, leading to Jessie's performance with the driftwood."

Dr. Raymond Blake, Canine Cultural Heritage Researcher:

"The boxer is a descendent of the Bullenbeiser Mastiff used in animal-baiting rings from the seventeenth to nineteenth centuries. These events, in which the dogs were pitted against a bear or another dog, were violent and bloody, the atmosphere one of tension and aggression. The dogs were caged in small stone enclosures around the perimeter of the ring behind an iron-barred door that was lowered into position to prevent escape. It was in these tight cold prisons that the Bullenbeiser dogs waited their stint in the ring, and were returned to if they were fortunate enough to survive the encounter. These savage and frequently brutal experiences were indelibly imprinted on the psyches of the dogs involved. Given a strong enough trigger, fragments of these memories passed down through generations will emerge in what seems to be a peculiar behavior.

"In Jessie's case, the two large stones in close proximity elicited the memory of her ancestors' ringside cages. The placement of the wooden lintels as a symbolic roof completed the stone enclosure, and the dog then settled beneath to await whatever would occur. The dog appeared neither aggressive nor fearful, which indicates that she was unaware of the significance of the structure and that the inherited fragment, purely visual, held no psychological component."

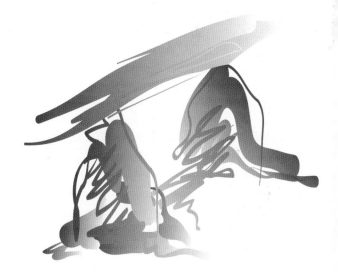

If you asked her, Jemima would probably regard her early experience of living with four young children as the pinnacle of mind-altering episodes. She has been unalterably scarred by that first meeting with small humans and now avoids them at all costs. Happily, she was rescued by her beloved owner Clive, but this was only the start of a life fraught with close encounters of the scariest kind.

Some dogs seek adventure; others have it thrust upon them. Jemima is both sorts of dog. As a close companion to a research biologist, she must be courageous and intrepid at all times. She's battled possums, involuntarily explored the bottom of an old mine, lodged herself in rabbit holes, and, most alarming of all, has been lost at sea. On a paddle crab expedition, Jemima—all decked out in a lurid pink life jacket and feeling omnipotent—leaned too far over the stern. Luckily, she was observed floating a few hundred feet behind the boat like an agitated blanc-mange, all four legs wildly flapping above the waves.

Jemima
A Corgi - Sheltie Mix
. . . .

Jemima is fondly referred to as Jemima Snappy Beak or Foxy Fagin due to her less-than-sociable manner with other dogs and her propensity to hunt small creatures. With the passing of the years and the slight blunting of her faculties, Jemima's personality has softened. She has a serenity about her and is beginning to regard other dogs much like a dowager bemused by a teenagers' party.

Jemima's creative endeavors, notably the symmetrical lines of windswept sand sculptures, were the catalyst to this study of canine construction. While we had photographed her finished work, we had yet to experience her creative process.

The beach we chose for Jemima's performance was prone to strong winds and rapid sand movement and we were concerned that these conditions would be overtaxing for her, given that she is fourteen years old, has extremely short legs, and would be working at ankle level. However, we were assured that once Jemima was involved in hole-digging pursuits, such environmental and anatomical obstacles would be of no significance to her.

The positioning of the sand-nests was obviously of paramount importance; after finishing each hollow, Jemima would look to her owner for a moment, snuffle about in an attempt to line up the existing holes, and suddenly throw herself into vigorous digging. Once each hole was completed the dog climbed into the sand crater and revolved a few times before stomping off to begin the next.

Dr. Raymond Blake, Canine Cultural Heritage Researcher:
"At first glance this dog's work seems to be a series of holes, but her habit of revolving and nestling in each hollow before moving on to the next structure indicates an intention to build a nest.

"On the Island of Voeroy canine researcher Sigurd Skaun has discovered an ancient, pure Nordic breed, a corgi-like spitz known as the Puffin Dog used for wild fowling for centuries. The crossbreeding of sheltie to corgi is of particular interest as it is clear that both breeds were descended from dogs involved with the feather and bird-egg trades several centuries ago

in Europe and the British outlying islands.

"Certainly the observation of two dogs of similar ancestry building nest-like structures must be more than merely a random coincidence. The trigger to Jemima's nest-building appears to be the proximity of the sea and the presence of sea birds in the vicinity."

Penelope Winter, Animal Spiritualist and Telepathic Diviner:

"Clive and Jemima have an unusually close relationship. Clive's decision to leave the army and take up a new career path coincided with the traumatic breakup of his marriage. Jemima entered his life as a small needy pup and they battled through several difficult years together. Their bond is almost tangible. The little dog is constantly checking on her owner and frequently reacts to thoughts barely formed in Clive's mind.

"At first, I was mystified by the dog's focus on the straightness of lines and symmetry of form. I asked Clive to stay out of sight during the digging of hole number four to see how much, if any, influence was being brought to bear on the placement of the sand nest. As I had presumed, Clive's absence made absolutely no difference. Telepathy does not require physical proximity. This type of thought transference is based on approval, and Jemima's entire purpose in life is to please her beloved master. Clive's obsession with order and straight lines, a direct influence from his army background, has been communicated to this little dog. Symmetry has become a major feature of her work."

The sandstorm gathered momentum during the final stage of Jemima's work and within minutes, the holes took on the appearance of softly eroded hollows surrounded by silky banks of pale grey sand.

Perching beside her sand nests after her performance, Jemima wore an introspective expression evocative of Puffin Dogs of a bygone era—or perhaps it was merely the effect of the fine sand adhering to her face?

In 1871 Lewis Morgan stated in The American Beaver and His Works *that he believed that beavers' dam-building behavior was a product of intellect, not instinct. The beaver conceives and executes a complex design, conscious of problems it solves through the exercise of reason. Charles Darwin disagreed. He maintained that it is the power of instinct that produces behavior that at first sight looks amazingly resourceful.*

Later experiments by modern scientists discovered that beavers are irritated by the sound of running water. In laboratory tests they try to escape it. When the sound of water was played on a stereo they attempted to dam the speaker! The inborn message is: if it's noisy, dam it. But how does this explain the engineering and architectural abilities displayed by beavers?

To Native Americans, the behavior of the beaver suggests a version of the creation myth. Beavers alter the landscape and control the waters in a most impressive way for such a small animal.

Shadow
A Black Labrador
. . . .

Shadow is a sleek black extrovert with a gregarious approach to life. His two absolute passions are water and his owner. Labradors, originally from Newfoundland, were known as the "little water dogs"; to a dog of this breed water is as elemental as the air he breathes. One of the most commonly held visual images of a Labrador is that of a dog leaping into a river to retrieve a stick or a duck, purely for the joy of its cool wetness.

Shadow is unique in his behavior regarding water: he refuses to retrieve, preferring instead to carry branches and sticks into the water as material with which to build.

Jane, Shadow's Owner:
"Shad has only recently started building bridges in the water. About three

months ago he was loafing about in the river and a water rat or something similar shot out of the branches on the river bank. Shad seemed mesmerized, and then he started grabbing branches and sticks and dragging them across the stream."

Dr. Raymond Blake, Canine Cultural Heritage Researcher:
"In all my studies of genetically transmitted behaviors, I must say that this is the first Labrador I have encountered who builds dams. Labradors are strong swimmers with short powerful limbs and were probably used by fishermen to carry rope ashore on the shelving beaches. Sea, nets, and boats are all part of the Labradors' genetic memory. Almost without exception, dogs of this breed show ecstatic response to any activity involving water. Retrieving from water is second nature to them.
"This dog however, *builds* in water.
"I requested a copy of the dog's pedigree and found that his great-grand-sire was imported from Sault Ste. Marie, Canada. Once we contacted the breeder, Shadow's behavior began to be decipherable. His great-grand-sire, Broc, lived with a research zoologist who was involved in a five-year

study of the life cycle and habits of the Canadian Brown Beaver. According to his breeder, Broc had an obsessive fascination with the dam constructions of these animals and persisted in trying to join the beavers in their building—much to the consternation of the beavers and the frustration of the zoologist.

"Of course, Shadow has never been to Canada, let alone observed a beaver in action. Nevertheless, the inherited memory of his ancestor's experience seems to have been triggered by the sighting of the water rat. It is almost as though a slide of beaver-building were projected onto the cortex of Shadow's brain, prompting him into constructing dams. The next step is to research Broc's other descendants to ascertain whether this genetic echo is shared or Shadow-specific."

Penelope Winter, Animal Spiritualist and Telepathic Diviner:
"At first glance it does appear that Shadow is building dams, and on a physical plane you could say that's exactly what he is doing. But the physical is merely an illusion. It's more important to ask, what does a dam signify from a symbolic point of view? It can mean protection or an obsta-

cle. Psychologically and symbolically it can refer to a need to limit, suppress, or prevent something from happening.

"I'm not clear if Shad is acting out his own needs or fears or is in fact reflecting his owner's stage in spiritual evolution. Shadow's repeated creation of these physical manifestations may be an attempt to help his owner confront her karmic learning. It is becoming increasingly clear that our relationships with animals as well as humans are not coincidental. We come together at various stages of our spiritual journey and these associations have a higher purpose."

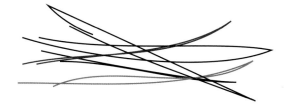

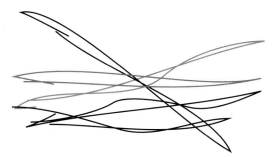

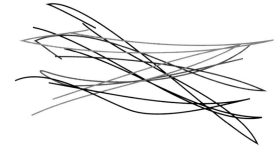

Moths, planes, birds—any winged intruder encroaching on the airspace above the farmhouse or garden drives Dash into a frenzy. She is self-appointed air traffic controller of the skies surrounding her territory. Even when dozing peacefully in the shade, Dash has her paw on the pulse of the flight paths of the winged: faster than the speed of light, this little Border is on her feet and escorting the flyers out of her property. She is convinced that it is her frantic barking that induces intruders to move away from her piece of sky and into the neutral zone.

Dash's confidence was seriously tested one evening when visiting children launched their kites in the adjoining field. The prevailing wind held the kites hovering about twelve feet above her head, and there they stayed. Dash's focus was on a bright yellow kite in the shape of a threatening-looking chicken. Suddenly the wind dropped and the chicken dive-bombed the terrified dog. It was nearly a week before Dash regained her equilibrium and resumed her role as Sheriff of the Skies.

Dash
A Border Collie
. . . .

Jack's body was found at daybreak, just as the sun began to whisper across the peaks of the gravel heaps in the quarry. Huddled against his oilskin-clad form was his Border Collie, Dash.

Jack's farm adjoins a large and potentially treacherous quarry face where sheep occasionally wander at night. This evening had been particularly stormy and ominous, prompting the farmer to check the area for animals in danger of slipping down the rocky face onto the gravel piles below. When he and his dog failed to return, his family put out an alarm. Seven hours later the tragedy was discovered.

Following the death of her friend, Dash showed all the usual signs of dog grief. However, she eventually recovered her exuberant high spirits and appeared to transfer her affections, bonding closely with Jack's widow, Friar.

We had heard about Dash in a letter from Friar: "My Border Collie regularly builds pyramids out of raincoats, but only at sunset when the weather is stormy and wet."

We arranged to meet Dash and Friar at the quarry adjoining their farm. The forecast was for a heavy rainstorm, clearing by evening, but these conditions failed to materialize and Dash simply refused to perform. She completely ignored the oilskin raincoats we had placed nonchalantly on the quarry floor, and we had to accept that another visit would be necessary. She clearly could not be baited or forced.

During the filming in the quarry, Dash appeared almost melancholy, with a wistful, reflective expression in her eyes. Friar said this only occurred at this location; Dash was usually true to her name, a maniacally energetic little dog who galloped about—a truly jubilant jet-propelled personality.

As we left the gravel heaps we noticed that the dog's spirits lifted—it was as though the memory of her beloved owner's death was firmly relegated to a hidden place in her mind and only activated by visiting the site of the tragedy.

Dr. Raymond Blake, Canine Cultural Heritage Researcher:
"The Border Collie, believed to be a descendant of a cross between Viking reindeer herders and Scottish sheepdogs, is so named for its popularity as a superb sheepdog in the border counties of England and Scotland. Dash's raincoat sculptures are reminiscent of the rocky outcrops so prevalent in that area of the British Isles. Additionally, it was common custom when caught in a sudden rainstorm for the shepherd to huddle with his dog beneath a makeshift oilskin tent.

However, after observing this dog's body language and mood swings I have to acknowledge that there seems to be an emotional trigger for her behavior. She may be suffering from a form of post-traumatic stress disorder and is reenacting the quarry tragedy. Faced with the same venue and similar cues—post-rainstorm, sunset, and oilskin coats—she is compelled to replay and thus relive the original trauma. As the dog is so site-specific, I suggest this as the most likely explanation."

Penelope Winter, Animal Spiritualist and Telepathic Diviner:

"Friar tells me that she and Jack first met in Egypt while both were on holiday. They fell in love, and Friar followed Jack back to his farm in the high country. Judging from the many framed photographs of the young couple set against the backdrop of the pyramids, this was a very special time and place for them. After Jack's death and more specifically on wet blustery evenings, Friar would gaze at the photographs and go into a kind of trance where she felt as though Jack's spirit were present in the room. Dash was always beside Friar during these sessions, and I am convinced that she is trying to communicate with and comfort Friar by reconstructing the pyramids out of oilskins."

Friar, Dash's Owner.

"I have never been very connected to the farm dogs, but Dash is different. During those times when I was communing with Jack and looking back at our first meeting and the romantic time we shared in Egypt, I felt that Dash and I were locked in a shared time bubble which rendered the real world irrelevant and incapable of intruding upon our thoughts."

Shylo was the firstborn of a beagle litter of six. Tragically, her brothers and sisters did not survive. She appears to have inherited the energy normally shared by the entire litter, and meets each day with great gusto. Perhaps she is aware of her extraordinary luck in being alive.

Beagles, originally only nine inches high, were very popular with the British monarchy from the 1300s to 1400s. They were known as Glove or Pocket Beagles as they were small enough to fit on the palm of one's hand. The name Beagle has two possible origins. It either came from the Celtic word beag, "small" or from the French word begle, "useless or of little value."

Shylo would certainly not subscribe to the second suggested derivative, as she is very certain of her worth and position in the world. She is a confident, self-possessed dog with a distinct mission: seeking out and tracking down smells. "Have nose—will discover" is her motto.

Shylo
A Purebred Beagle
· · · · · · · · · · · · · · · ·

My young beagle Shylo hangs socks on the fence! We have four beagles and all love playing with socks, but Shylo is the only one who does the fence thing. Our neighbor, a retired army officer, plays his bugle quite frequently in the early evening, and the sound of the horn seems to trigger Shylo to hang out her socks.

—Excerpt from owner's letter.

Dr. Raymond Blake, Canine Cultural Heritage Researcher:
"The crucial questions in explaining this dog's behavior are: Why socks? What is the connection with the bugle? And why only one of the four dogs? I discovered a possible link in the obscure writings of a retired English huntsman. After the hunt, while the adults were replenishing their vigor with hip flasks of whisky, the children would play 'Pin the Tail

on the Child.' This game required each child to hang an article of clothing—a sock or a glove for instance—on a fence. At the sound of the horn, their chosen hound was sent in to retrieve the article. The child whose hound was first to bring back the correct item won the game and was entitled to wear the fox's tail pinned to his or her jacket.

"Beagles are traditionally used in hunting hares, not foxes. After extensive research into Shylo's ancestry, we discovered that her predecessors came from a breeding kennel where a small pack of beagles accompanied the fox hounds on hunts—an eccentric break with tradition on the part of the huntsman. This could explain why the other beagles in Shylo's household do not share the inherited memory of the foxtail game."

Penelope Winter, Animal Spiritualist and Telepathic Diviner:
"I think Dr. Blake's explanation seems rather farfetched. To me the socks on the fence resemble musical notes. At first I wondered if Shylo was recreating the music of the neighbor's bugle, but the placement of the notes didn't match the bugle's tunes. While building her sculpture, Shylo continually put her head to one side as though listening to sounds in the far distance. I believe that she is hearing the music of her ancestors' voices or the singing of the wind in the trees."

Minka is a seven-year-old Standard Poodle with an impeccable pedigree. Somehow, due to the genetic mix or strong influence from her very distant wolf ancestor, she has yellow eyes. This gives her a slightly feral appearance at odds with her poodle elegance and curls.

Living with Minka is never boring. She has a quirky sense of humor and is a lateral thinker. This has frequently proved to be disastrous in her career as an obedience competition dog, since she continually invents increasingly outrageous alternatives to the set exercises. Minka's pièce de résistance occurred during a scent discrimination test: she selected her cloth, stood with her paws on her hips looking defiant, and finally jumped out of the ring to deliver the scent cloth to her litter brother, who was competing in another event.

Life for Minka is a continuous party, and Golden Retrievers are the icing on the cake. Her burning passion for Goldies, although awesome to behold, is sometimes embarrassing for the recipients of her attentions. Also on her list of desirables are pumpkin skins, feathers, and men with Dutch accents.

Minka
A Standard Poodle
. . . .

The acquisition of feathers has been Minka's major raison d'être since, as a pup of ten weeks old, she first discovered their joyful properties. From that first ecstatic sensory-loaded moment she has considered them unsurpassed as a material to gather, arrange, chew upon, and spend quality time with.

Strangely, Minka appears unconcerned that the feathers that come into her possession are no longer attached to a bird. In fact birds hold very little interest for her as long as they retain ownership of the coveted feathers. Until very recently Minka's activity with feathers had been relatively random. She had poked them unceremoniously into bushes, gathered them into small bushy piles, and occasionally laid them out for inspection. Watching the dog's movements one evening, her owner, Rebecca Francois, began to focus on the placement of several white turkey feathers Minka had just acquired.

"It was quite eerie—all of a sudden Minka stopped batting the feathers about and sat motionless, staring at me intently. To my total amazement, she then placed one of the feathers in the exact position I had been thinking of. After Minka had arranged four feathers almost exactly where I'd envisaged them, I started thinking about whether this could be a sort of telepathic communication. The moment I considered this idea, Minka stalked off to lie under a bush, holding the last feather in her mouth." With the cooperation of Minka's owner, we transported dog and feathers to a beach to observe what, if any, response she would show. Our hope was that Rebecca and Minka would be able to recreate the previous experience of thought transference, but Minka quickly leapt upon her pile of feathers with gay abandon and set about composing a floating sculpture in the tidal pond.

Dr. Raymond Blake, Canine Cultural Heritage Researcher:
"It was indeed intriguing to observe this poodle involved with collecting and transporting feathers in such a focused manner. It brought to mind a historic text that referred to a nineteenth-century count in the province of Touraine who used poodle retrievers in a rather novel way: At the end of a day's shoot the poodles were given one feather from each bird and sent back to the castle. These feathers were presented to the cook, thus

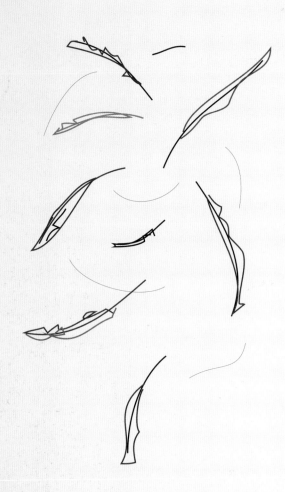

alerting the kitchen staff as to the number and type of birds requiring culinary attention upon the shooting party's return.

"It is recorded that a male puppy from the count's kennels was gifted to a visiting English duke who was impressed by the poodles' quick intelligence and independence. The duke's youngest brother, an early immigrant to New Zealand, was accompanied by two of the offspring of the male French Poodle. After extensive research we traced Minka's genealogy and found that she was directly related to the great-granddaughter of the union between these two immigrants from England. Minka obviously carries the genetic memory of her distant ancestors. It appears that the trigger for the dog's feather-transporting behavior is the presence of a substantial heap that activates the recall of dead ducks piled together. Part of the memory is missing: while the dog knows that she must transport the feathers, she appears at a loss as to where they should be delivered. Given the nonexistence of a castle, this is hardly surprising."

Penelope Winter, Animal Spiritualist and Telepathic Diviner:
"I was fascinated by Minka's exquisite arrangement of feathers in the sea pond. Initially she worked haphazardly and seemingly without intention, and the feathers gave the appearance of a crash-landing site of an entire flock of turkeys. However, she then went into a trance and stood among the confusion of feathers, staring intently. After a few minutes of contemplation she began quite deliberately and selectively removing large

groups of feathers and returning them to the banks of the pool. Once satisfied, Minka ran off down the beach in search of a Golden Retriever she had spotted earlier.

"I didn't feel that Minka was trying to communicate with her owner or acting on a telepathic connection with Rebecca. Either she was entranced with the visual quality of a kinetic art form or, more likely, she was receiving instructions from a psychic source. My assumption that she was contemplating may be wrong; perhaps she was meditating while awaiting further directions from another plane.

"I did wonder if the floating design, with its almost geometric appearance, may have been some kind of spiritual revelation. But the fact that Minka kept changing it was confusing. Perhaps that was the message—an insightful observation on the ever-changing nature of the planet?"

There is a side to Emily that doesn't seem to fit with her tough exterior and her obsession with mud and bones. She has an extremely sophisticated appreciation of cultural matters—particularly music. Not your "down on the farm" country-and-western taste for Emily. Her great passion is to lie between the stereo speakers in the evening, eyes half-closed, relaxing to the strains of Schubert, Bach, and—above all—Vivaldi. The Four Seasons sends this little dog into a state of such stupefied ecstasy that her owner Liz, afraid that Emily will become permanently comatose, must limit the playing time.

Emily and Liz do not always see eye-to-eye in the choice of compact discs.

"I'm really into '70s music. While Emily will tolerate the Eagles and Joan Armatrading, her preference is clearly classical. She can put on a very sinister expression when her favorite CDs have to give way to my selection of music."

On the odd occasion when the piano lid is left open, inside there can be found small muddy marks that look suspiciously like paw prints.

Emily
A Staffordshire Bull Terrier
· · · · · · · · · · · · · · · · ·

E mily is a powerhouse of energy, muscle, and grins. She is equally ecstatic perched on the lap of her owner, Liz, or clinging precariously to the seat of a speeding farm bike.

Emily's fascination with bones is renowned in the farming district in which she lives. Cow bones are her preference, and she's often observed scurrying about the carcass pits on neighboring properties, adding to her personal bone stockpile. This in itself is not remarkable; dogs and bones are intrinsically connected. But Emily's drive for bone collecting verges on the extraordinary.

Liz, Emily's owner

"The first time we observed Emily working with her bones was in midwinter, when the paddock was a sea of mud from the trampling of a herd of beef cattle. She was sitting beside her latest collection, staring with intent at the different bone shapes. As we watched she made her choice and stomped out into the mud carrying a saber-shaped rib bone. A moment later she was back to the pile and the staring began again. After four bones had been transported to the mud site we crept closer, intrigued. There in the mud was an oval shape made up of eight bones gleaming in the sunlight against a background of black cow-trampled bog. Several times that winter, Emily engaged in building similar structures. "We did wonder about the cattle's peace of mind as they observed the little staffie tromping about their paddock carrying body parts of long-departed friends and relatives!"

—Excerpt from owner's letter.

Speculating that mud was an important ingredient in Emily's composition, and in deference to the cattle's comfort, we met Liz and Emily at a mudflat at low tide. Emily surpassed herself that evening and produced three bone circles. Her excitement at having an audience may explain the repetition of her usual single construction.

Penelope Winter, Animal Spiritualist and Telepathic Diviner:
"I'm interested in the relationship between Emily and her owner. I perceive a strong physic link particularly evident prior to the placing of each bone in the circle. Emily, on reaching the circle site, pauses and inclines her head in Liz's direction before actually positioning the bone. There is no obvious body-language signal between human and dog and it does not

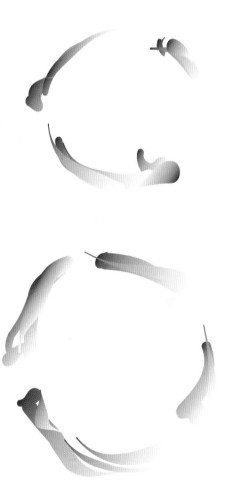

seem as though Emily is seeking approval. After all, her first bone sculpture was built without an acknowledged audience. It's possible that the first composition, observed from a distance, may have been relatively random; Liz's designer's background made sense of the scattered bones, and from that point unconsciously transferred circle visualizations to the dog. "However, I do see another possibility. The circle signifies the cyclical nature of cosmology. Historically, time was seen to move through cycles; death was merely a point on the circular spiritual journey. Animals certainly haven't evolved a concept of linear time. The circle is as much part of their consciousness as it was for cultures of many centuries ago. Making rings of bones could be an extension of Emily's inherent consciousness of the cyclical nature of the physical and spiritual cosmos."

Dr. Raymond Blake, Canine Cultural Heritage Researcher: "The dog's owner belongs to a Dianic Pagan group that concentrates on women's mysteries and the goddess aspect. This particular branch of the Dianic path reveres *Arianhod* (silver wheel), the goddess of reincarnation. The silver wheel represents the circumpolar stars, which never set below the horizon. This is the resting-place to which souls were believed to withdraw between incarnations.

"In some parts of Britain, pagan high priests were accompanied by a type of dog not unlike the precursor to the Staffordshire Bull Terrier. These dogs were included in the pagan rituals, as it was believed that only dogs go through to the afterlife. The dogs' function was to choose the bones to be used for the ritual circle. Emily comes from an old, established line of British Staffordshire Bull Terriers. She escorts her owner to her monthly Dianic meetings, where the circle or silver wheel is formed by rocks of

quartz derivation or sun-bleached bones. I believe that this dog is responding to reverberations from a bygone era when her ancestors were intimately involved with bone circles. Emily's owner's group and their use of cow bones have sparked her peculiar behavior."

Emily, very popular with the Dianic group, has been appointed an honorary member. She takes a great interest in the arrangement of the bones at each meeting place.

Flossie's suspected high intellect is veiled by her rather scattered and overexcited reaction to the rich tapestry of life. When just a young pup she was hit by a speeding car and in a blind panic disappeared for five days; she had sought refuge in a large drainage pipe several miles from the accident site. When finally rescued by the fire department she was distressed, cold, and hungry, and had a badly injured leg. Since this traumatic experience, Flossie (understandably) views life as a minefield. The slightest unusual sound throws her into an anxiety attack.

With empathetic handling and well-established routines she was weaned off medication and now has an exceptionally close relationship with her owners. Once you are introduced to and approved of by Flossie, you have a friend for life. She recognizes even fleeting acquaintances from a great distance and throws herself into a greeting with an enthusiasm almost daunting to behold.

Flossie
A Wheaten Terrier
. . . .

After reading an article about human/canine telepathy, with absolute faith in Flossie's innate intelligence her owner Grant decided to attempt a thought-transference exercise involving the concept of triangles. This instead proved to be an exercise in extreme bewilderment for Flossie and a frustrating experience for her owner. Finally, both owner and dog agreed to disagree on the significance and importance of placing sticks *anywhere*—let alone forming a triangle.

Flossie is an inveterate bone-burier. She lives in the garden of a market and her favorite site for burying and excavating is a huge pile of fine wood chips used for bedding plants. Several weeks after Grant's abortive attempt to educate Flossie on the joys of triangles, he noticed that the dog was still carrying her bones to the chip pile—but once she interred them

she did not dig them up again. This was entirely out of character. Grant visited Flossie's "burial site" and found three mounds of wood chips. While Flossie looked on with an enigmatic expression—not part of her usual repertoire of facial distortions—Grant excavated the first mound and found three meticulously cleaned white bones placed in the configuration of a triangle. Random coincidence? Pure chance? Investigation of the other two mounds revealed the same story: three bones placed in a triangle.

Penelope Winter, Animal Spiritualist and Telepathic Diviner:
"Now this is quite unusual but not unknown: telepathy or thought transference deflected and then applied to a completely different situation. Although at the time it seemed to Grant that there was no telepathic con-

nection, Flossie received the message loud and clear. However, colored sticks were not her choice of materials and were completely irrelevant to her own agenda. I think the owner's obvious frustration with his dog was an obstacle to free-flowing psychic communication. Once the dog was in a tranquil environment, she accessed the transferred information and used it in her own way. Triangles are universal symbols for a desire for stability. Flossie is an insecure, anxious little dog and is dependent on her owners for a sense of equilibrium. Triangles obviously have a lot of significance for her."

Dr. Raymond Blake, Canine Cultural Heritage Researcher:
" 'Free-flowing psychic communication?' There was absolutely no indication of thought transference happening with this dog. Wheaten Terriers are indigenous to Ireland, and Flossie's direct ancestry can be traced back to Drogheda, County Meath. Six miles west of the town are nineteen passage graves and numerous standing stones, henges, and barrows. The chambers and curbstones have been elaborately carved with spirals, chevrons, and triangles. This dog's great-grandmother belonged to an archaeologist who carbon-dated the relics found at the sites and investi-

gated the symbolic significance of the marks on the stones. The dog accompanied him on his prolonged visits to the sites. Several archaeological researchers have concluded that the triangles depict the fields of wheat so vital to the survival of the middle–Stone Age people in that area. Both the stone-carved symbols and the distinctive triangular-shaped fields are imprinted on the genetic memory of Wheaten Terriers from this part of the county.

"Another explanation lies in the use of Wheaten Terriers by the Irish as hunters. Like most terriers they are extremely fond of rat catching, and this inherent talent was utilized by their owners both to control vermin and to add excitement to their often joyless lives in the form of rat-killing competitions. Each dog was given a set amount of time to kill as many rats as possible in a designated area—usually a grain store or feed barn. The dead rats were then laid out in threes in the form of a triangle so that it was easy for the counter to work out how many rats had been caught by each dog.

"Flossie encounters mice and rats regularly in the compost bins of the market's garden. Due to her nervous temperament she leaves them to their scavenging, but genetically she is programmed to attack. Placing her bones in triangles is her way of accessing these memories via her ancestors."

One of Buck's earliest memories is his encounter with a red scooter on his first journey outside the safety of his backyard. Trotting confidently and briskly, he was halfway over the pedestrian crossing when out of nowhere appeared a flash of red and the squealing of wheels. Buck ended up beneath the scooter. While uninjured, he was traumatized. It is possible that the visual combination of black and white spots moving across the crossing's white and black stripes momentarily confused the rider of the scooter; he was adamant that he hadn't seen the pup at all.

Buck's reaction to this disturbing event was profound. Apart from his fear of moving vehicles (which has persisted throughout adulthood), he became listless and nervy, and seemed to lose his zest for life. He was treated by vets, homeopaths, and dog psychologists to no avail. Finally, despite the skepticism of his owner, Buck visited a color therapist who focused on the color red in an attempt to restore his confidence and vital energy. Buck responded and bounced back to his former animated self.

Buck
A Purebred Dalmatian
. . . .

Dalmatians have been circus performers, gundogs, military sentinels, and retrievers, but mostly they are known as carriage or fire-truck dogs. Their job was to run either in front of the horses or between the wheels of the horse-drawn carriage—an unnecessary act of bravery, judging by Buck's attitude to both horses and moving vehicles.

Dr. Raymond Blake, Canine Cultural Heritage Researcher:
"This dog does not seem to have inherited an attraction for vehicles, but visual echoes from the experiences of his ancestors are activated whenever he comes across tires—as long as they remain stationary. I am not certain why he has the need to then fill the inner space of the tire with vegetables. According to his owner Buck was a vegetarian as a young dog due to digestive problems. This was resolved but the dog is still curiously

attached to raw vegetables as playthings. Perhaps he is merely combining the two in a desire to contain and hoard his favorite objects. It is interesting that given the choice, Buck will always select red vegetables or objects to place in his tire containers. Possibly the dog is recreating an image of a fire engine, as the black wheels with glimpses of red would be his main focus from his position alongside the truck."

Penelope Winter, Animal Spiritualist and Telepathic Diviner:
"I don't believe that the tire itself is significant, since Buck is still wary of vehicles. I think that the circular tire containing smaller circles, in this case vegetables, is a symbol or code that we humans are struggling to understand. When finished with his constructions, Buck stands still and eyeballs his audience intently, as though willing them to get the message. I believe that while dogs are supposedly colorblind, they do distinguish tones. If Buck is recreating anything, I think it's his own interpretation of a spotted dalmatian—but a brightly colored one, as he would wish to be.
"Bucks's attraction to the color or tone of red can certainly be associated with his treatment by the color therapist. Red objects would revitalize him and give him a sense of confidence and well-being."

Alaskan Malamutes can be traced back to the Mahlemut tribe inhabiting Alaska, and it is believed that they are descended from the Arctic wolf.

Luke is a powerful, imposing-looking dog. He has a mostly gentle and playful temperament and largely complies with what is expected of him as a domestic dog living in a small rural community. However, his wolf ancestry lurks beneath the surface: at times he freezes in a state of exquisite stillness, as though he is receiving messages on the wind or hearing the rustle of ancient times undetectable by human ears. On these occasions his expression is chilling—yet, in a strange way, inspiring. Despite the Alaskan Malamute's reputation of being fond of fighting with other dogs, Luke's gentle side triumphs when socializing at dog obedience school. Watching the 130-pound dog crawling about with puppies is heartwarming.

Luke
An Alaskan Malamute
. . . .

Luke's owners contacted us with an intriguing story of the dog's relationship to pampas grass. Mark had cut down a rampant growth of the plant from the border of his property and piled the soft, cream-colored heads near Luke's kennel until he could dispose of them. Luke appeared only mildly interested, but this changed dramatically when Mark visited the dog that evening. As is their ritual, he sang a special moon-baying song, expecting Luke to join in. To his amazement Luke leapt into the midst of the pampas pile and one by one extracted seven heads, placing them in a pattern on the lawn. Checking on the dog later that night, Mark found him lying among the pampas heads as they gleamed softly in the moonlight. The following evening Luke's owners set the scene again and waited in vain for some response.

But the next night, when Mark went out for his nightly duet, Luke again began seizing the heads and arranging them—this time in a different pattern. His owner concluded that his singing must be the trigger, but the dog's motivation remained a mystery.

Dr. Raymond Blake, Canine Cultural Heritage Researcher:
"Luke is a direct descendant of a female Malamute from the British Antarctic survey project. The last team left the Antarctic on February 22, 1994. Sadly, there are very few descendants of these talented dog teams; once outside the sterile conditions of the pole, the dogs fell victim to many diseases. Breeding programs have largely been unsuccessful. The dogs' 'singing' was very important. It gave direction to other teams, or signaled to a lost dog or human. When humans made a similar howling call, the dogs would answer. Singing was also an important part of the dogs' social order; they would sing just before they settled down for the evening. Each dog has a slightly different pitch. When a team are in full voice together they have a choral quality, and their 'hymns' evoke an ancient, mysterious past.

"The pampas-grass configuration we observed is curiously reminiscent of the fan-trace arrangement of a dog team. One lead dog followed by three pairs, all attached to separate lines. This was done to prevent the entire team from being pulled into a crevasse should one unfortunate dog fall through the ice.

"The pampas heads, I believe, are symbolic of the powerful bushy tails of sled-dog breeds. This explains why this dog requires both the singing trigger and the visual cue of the pampas grass to access his inherited memory. He then lies within the fan-trace configuration as though part of the dog team. Another pattern he has arranged is that of seven pampas stalks in a line. This may represent the night span in which the dogs are positioned every evening prior to feeding and sleeping."

Penelope Winter, Animal Spiritualist and Telepathic Diviner: "Why would Luke need to hear a human singing like a dog to trigger his psychic memory? He could do that perfectly well on his own. There must be a connection between Mark's communication with Luke and Luke's immediate response. I think it's much more likely that Luke is trying to reveal some kind of message to his owners. Because humans are not very good at reading animals' attempts to communicate on a telepathic level, Luke feels that he must express himself on a physical plane.

"Dogs of Luke's breed are believed to be closely related to the wolf and as we know, the wolf is said to embody the Teacher and the Pathfinder. I think Luke is spending this life with these owners for a significant reason and has spiritual wisdom to impart to them. Each pampas stalk represents a pathway to new beginnings. At the time of Luke's attempts at commu-

nication his owners were in a quandary about their direction in life. They were feeling trapped and disenchanted and this was making Luke feel uncomfortable. I believe that this dog's message to his owners is to stop running around in ever decreasing circles and to look at taking positive steps into the future."

Titch was placed in an animal shelter at four years of age. Due to renovations at the rescue center, all the canine inhabitants were transported to the local pound each night. The conditions at the pound were reminiscent of a prison camp. Titch's rather daunting appearance and the knowing look in her eyes earned her single-dog accommodation, but the rest of the dogs were housed in one large caged area. Every morning the shelter workers found a dead dog or one badly mutilated from the inevitable violent fights for supremacy. After a week, many of the dogs were so traumatized that new homes could not be found for them. Titch, whose method of coping with the ordeal was apparently to detach herself from the events, was adopted by Bella, the animal-shelter officer. Seven years later, Titch shows very few signs of lasting effects from that period in her life. She is composed, aloof, and above all, passionately devoted to her rescuer.

Titch
A Rottweiler-Labrador Mix

· · · · · · · · · · · · · · · ·

Titch draws.

She draws with formidable intensity of focus and design and has a wide repertoire of techniques ranging from vigorous linear marks to soft, sensitive lines overlaid by sweeping curves. Her only requirements are a suitable drawing tool and a firm but yielding surface for her canvas.

Titch's strong will is reflected in her work. She is a dog with a mission: once she begins to draw she continues unabated, ignoring any attempts at influencing either style or content.

Bella, Titch's Owner:

"I remember the first time Titch showed me how she could draw. About three weeks after I adopted her, she and I were sloping about at the beach, kicking up sand and paddling in the low tide. I picked up a stick and drew a large *T* for Titch, dropped the stick, and walked on. Titch shot back to the stick, fixed it between her front paws and drew a rather wobbly *I* beside the *T*. 'Unreal,' I thought, 'This dog can spell!' and drew another *T* next to Titch's *I*. I waited for the dog to put down a *C* but she seized the stick and went into a frenzy of lines and half-circles joined together with soft squiggly bits.

"Once I had recovered from my disappointment that she wasn't in fact an intellectual giant with a reading age of eight, I began to closely inspect her marks on the sand. It was very impressive for a first drawing and I started to suspect that she was actually an experienced artist and had been involved in beach art for quite some time. It was awesome to watch the transformation in the dog. I had been concerned because she seemed unemotional and lacking in the usual young-dog enthusiasm for life. But

this passion for drawing has continued for the past seven years and during that time she has never repeated a design. At times I wish she would paint on canvas so I could frame them for her!"

By chance, we found Titch and Bella on a beach; the dog was already intensely involved in her creative effort. With Titch's permission we set up our cameras and photographed her at work until the sun fell into the sea and Titch set down her stick beside her drawing.

Dr. Raymond Blake, Canine Cultural Heritage Researcher:

"Rottweilers were used extensively as droving dogs in Germany. To drove means to round up, control, move in different directions, dominate, intimidate, keep in LINE, enCIRCLE, keep intense focus, and enclose— a kind of kinetic art form.

"This dog's work encompasses all of these qualities. It is possible that she is using the stick to describe the droving patterns of her predecessors, although she wouldn't necessarily understand the connection.

"Alternately, and at the risk of being accused of anthropomorphism, we cannot ignore the dog's recent past experiences. Her behavior on sand with a stick is the only visible expression she shows of the shocking events she witnessed. The dog uses very aggressive and forceful marks when she is drawing, which may indicate unresolved feelings. Whereas the other dogs in the pound responded by becoming stupefied or hysterical, this dog shut off and escaped to some internal place to cope."

Penelope Winter, Animal Spiritualist and Telepathic Diviner:

"I cannot believe that Titch would express her feelings only when given a stick at the beach. There are countless opportunities for her to give vent to repressed emotions, but she does not. Also, there is no obvious connection between the beach and the dog-pound experience.

"I think it much more likely that she is in contact with a lower-level incarnate who has not yet come to terms with leaving the earth plane and is using Titch's work to vent its anguish.

"My spirit guide Madame Blavatsky tells me that this is so, and in our consultation gave me the names *Rottweil* and *Krux*. I have an aged aunt living in Rottweil and contacted her. According to local legend, in Rottweil in 1916 there lived an artist of the Dada movement who was known as a misogynist and a recluse; his only companion was his large black Rottweiler dog, Krux. The artist frequently forgot to feed the dog, and one fateful day Krux ate a crust lying in a pool of turpentine and died an unpleasant and violent death. The artist, riddled with guilt, died soon after. It's thought that he still inhabits areas of Rottweil, trapped between the physical world and the spiritual plane. I think it quite possible he is continuing his work through dogs of Krux's breeding.

"Titch appears to take on a different persona when drawing and is left drained and exhausted. The finished work is angry and aggressive and although I could not find any surviving examples of the Rottweil artist's work, the general appearance of Titch's drawing is very similar to works belonging to the Dada movement."

Kaysee is the boss in a household of seven dogs. She is the smallest, oldest, and seemingly the least interested in things hierarchical, yet she reigns supreme. To the human eye this diminutive Cairn Terrier gives no apparent signals to protect her position, but the rule is: don't mess with Kaysee.

It is difficult to imagine where she learned her skills. Kaysee was imported from the heart of cairn country, Inverness of Clava Cairns fame. Her mother went missing the days prior to whelping, and after a long and frustrating search four newborn puppies were found, nestled together for warmth beneath one of the portal stones surrounding Clava Cairns. Their mother was discovered an hour later, lying dead amidst a pile of small yellow stones on the outskirts of the area. The puppies were round and plump and remarkably unscathed by their traumatic start to life. All four survived hand-rearing and eventually were dispersed to their new homes and lives.

Kaysee
A Cairn Terrier
. . . .

Kaysee is a small, rotund Cairn Terrier with a passion for rocks. She relates to them with all of her senses: guards them, checks them out with her tongue, hugs them, listens as though they have a secret to tell, and rubs herself on their sun-warmed surfaces.

Nicki, Kaysee's Owner:
"We've always just accepted that Kaysee is into rocks. Since she was a small pup she's been devoted to them. It was so strange watching her cuddle up to the rocks in our garden and, transfixed, press her ear against their sides. Lately, though, her obsession with them has taken a new turn. In the park where we walk her, the river has undercut one of its banks and a pile of silver-colored rocks of enormous dimensions has been dumped there to prevent further erosion. Kaysee made a beeline for them, making the peculiar little crooning sound she reserves for rocks, and we left her to it.

"A cup of tea later we joined Kaysee on her pile and noticed a small yellow stone balanced on the pinnacle of one of the larger rocks. Kaysee watched us inspect it and to our astonishment disappeared behind the pile, returning with another yellow stone in her mouth. This in itself was strange, as picking up hard objects was not something she usually indulged in. She then shot up the side of a boulder and placed the small stone on the top. The second stone was more difficult to balance, but she persevered until it stayed in position. This was the beginning of Kaysee's new game. Since then, whenever she comes across small pebbles and large rocks she seems compelled to do this."

Dr. Raymond Blake, Canine Cultural Heritage Researcher:
"A cairn is a pile of stones or rocks used as markers or for ceremonial purposes. Fragments of skulls, limb bones, oak charcoal, and pottery shards have been found buried beneath them. They are often protected by rings of standing stones and were used as family shrines and places where sun and moon rituals and death rites were carried out.

"Cairn Terriers are aptly named, as historically their job was to keep the vermin away from the cairns and burial grounds. Like most terriers, their instinct to hunt small creatures is very strong.

"This dog's obsessive behavior around rocks indicates a strong link to her ancestors from Inverness. The whimpering sound her owner mentions would be in anticipation of finding rats and other vermin to excavate. The dog's trick of balancing small stones on the boulders is indeed strange, but I would hazard a guess that it is learned behavior. The first balanced stone received expressions of praise and delight. Dogs, ever keen to please their humans, could well have discovered very quickly that this trick was worth repeating.

"Another possibility is that this dog is recreating one of her first visual memories of the Clava Cairns. Viewed from a small pup's perspective the roof of the passage grave would give the appearance of large supporting boulders with small stones clustered on top."

Penelope Winter, Animal Spiritualist and Telepathic Diviner:
"Obviously Kaysee is not merely searching for rats, which is not high on her list of favorite activities. This little dog had an extremely traumatic introduction to life. Born in the shadow of the Clava portal stone and left motherless within hours of her birth would most definitely have a lasting

effect on her view of the world. Not only would she see the portal stone and, subsequently, any other large rock as a mother substitute, but the stone-circle symbolism would add to the intensity of her attraction. Stone circles are the cosmic eye of the great Goddess, the universal mother. The circle also depicts love for the mother, unity, and the unborn child.

"Kaysee is looking for her mother. She is trying to recreate the initial warmth and comfort she found under the Clava stone. The small yellow stones balancing on the boulders are marks of respect for her dead mother. Yellow is the spiritual color of death in some cultures, and stones, despite their hardness, are generally seen as lifegiving, not rigid or dead. They contain the essence of the Earth. The upright stones were placed to protect the dead from hostile powers. Perhaps Kaysee is ensuring this protection for her lost mother.

"Despite Dr. Blake's explanation of Kaysee's peculiar crooning sound, I believe the dog is connecting with the sound resonance from the rocks and is receiving energy from their vibrations. There is a frequency in that resonance that allows communication. While we humans have lost this sensitivity, animals are ever in tune with the energy of nature."

Abbie is a nurturer and befriender of small creatures. In the world of humans she is a rather aloof little dog; one must cultivate her respect and affection over time. However, the animals she takes under her wing are instantly loved and accepted by virtue of being small and in need. Her first mothering role involved a tiny, soft, prickled hedgehog that, lacking basic navigational skills, wandered into the kitchen. Abbie was enchanted and the two were inseparable until "Humphrey" remembered that he was in fact a hedgehog, and disappeared during the winter to hibernate. After an appropriate period of mourning, Abbie transferred her affections to Delia, a young duckling who was the sole survivor of a particularly treacherous duckling season. Their friendship endures.

Abbie
A Shetland Sheepdog
. . . .

The morning sun moved into position between the reeds, illuminating Abbie's cluster of pinecones and stones. We had agreed to meet Abbie and her owner on an island featuring an abundance of materials for her to use in building the nest structures for which she was renowned.

Dr. Raymond Blake, Canine Cultural Heritage Researcher:
"Initially I was perplexed by the connection between a herding dog such as the Shetland Sheepdog and her interest in nests and egg-shaped objects. But after research into the distant background of the breed, I found that the ancestors of the Shetland Sheepdog were from Scandinavia: known as Lundehunds, Peerie, or Fairy Dogs, they were carried aboard Icelandic fishing boats to both the Orkney and Shetland

Islands centuries ago. Fish, fowl, and eggs were the staple diet of both humans and dogs. Even more significant was the ancient trade in birds' eggs and feathers, the latter used to stuff the featherbeds of the wealthy. The instincts and specially adapted conformation of local dogs would have been ideal for seeking out seabird nests and their eggs and feathers. The feather trade spread from Nordic lands all over Europe, and there were annual peaceful Norse expeditions to the Scottish and Welsh coasts in search of the puffin bird and the eider duck. So my conclusion is that, unquestionably, this dog is reestablishing contact with her origins and acting out an inherited memory and behavior from centuries ago."

Penelope Winter, Animal Spiritualist and Telepathic Diviner:
"I don't see Abbie's work as representing nests at all. I think she collects objects and arranges them in clusters.

"Abbie is an ultra-self-contained personality. Scrupulously tidy, she is very attentive to minute detail. She lives with a Golden Retriever whose rather clumsy, untidy approach to life agitates her desire for order. Abbie's almost obsessive clustering of objects became much more developed after the retriever puppy joined the family. At first, her need to build groups of objects only arose in his presence. Now, however, she is galvanized into action whenever she is confronted with a collection of scattered objects. Her owner says that if Abbie were human she would be a fanatical housekeeper who would nag other members of the family into being the same."

Zeta is a dog of the night. Perhaps her dingo ancestry has a bearing on the way she sees the world, and in the deserts of Australia she would be at one with the rhythm of the land. Stars are of enormous fascination to Zeta. Reluctant to leave her shelter while the sun is in the sky, she disappears from the house each night, and most often can be found beside the creek gazing up at the constellations. Perhaps her behavior can be explained in part by the star stories of African and Aboriginal bushmen. They regard the stars as the great hunters whose hunting cries are far-off hissing sounds: "tssik" and "tsa." These are also the sounds African hunters use to alert their dogs to the presence of prey. Lauren Van De Post experimented with the star music on dogs outside of Africa, where these sounds were apparently unknown. In The Heart of the Hunter, *Van De Post claims that many responded with "that involuntary and nostalgic whimper normally provoked in them only by the moon." Dogs know these sounds; they learned them from the stars themselves.*

Zeta
An Australian Kelpie
. . . .

The dingo is a dog of mystery. It is not certain whether it is in fact a wild dog or one that has returned to the wild after domestication. The Australian bushmen believe that the Kelpie was originally a cross between a smooth-coated collie and a feral dingo. Certainly the Kelpies' appearance gives credence to this theory.

Zeta was born in the Australian outback. As a tiny potbellied pup with enormous pricked ears, her owners noticed that she frequently excluded herself from the company and games of her littermates and could be found gazing avidly at the evening sky. For the first six months of her life she was known as the "Star Pup." By the time she was sold to a family moving overseas, the name *Zeta* had somehow become attached to her. But no one—not even her owners—can remember or trace how this name came to be.

Now a mature eight-year-old, Zeta still has an intimate connection with the stars. She came to our attention via a letter from her owner, who wanted help in unraveling a mysterious behavior that had recently developed.

"My dog has started making crosses out of eucalyptus bark. It all began one evening when we decided to build a campfire to cook marshmallows. I had put down two sticks in preparation when Zeta rushed off to a pile of eucalyptus bark and constructed a similar cross structure. I thought she was just copying me, but she continued until there were three crosses in a line. What reason do you think she could have for doing this?"

—*Excerpt from owner's letter.*

Zeta almost missed out on being included in this book; we visited her on six different evenings over a period of five months to no avail. It was on the seventh occasion that her owner told us of her original name, Star

Pup, and we wondered if specific stars had to be visible in order to trigger Zeta's activity. To our delight, this happened to be *the* evening for Zeta's grand performance: the crosses were built almost at the speed of light. For Zeta's finale, she lay calm yet alert in the midst of her work.

Penelope Winter, Animal Spiritualist and Telepathic Diviner:

"I feel we have experienced a magic event with this dog, Zeta.

"I was convinced that the name *Star Pup* held the key, and then I received a strong message to look at the name *Zeta*. Of course! Zeta is one of the three stars forming the belt of Orion, the celestial hunter. The position of the Orion constellation in the sky may have some significance of which only animals connected to planetary changes would be aware.

"The Australian Aborigines use a cross symbol to indicate a star, and this dog with her dingo connections must be building Orion's belt using a similar symbol. Orion is accompanied by his two hunting dogs, Sirius and Procyon, making Zeta's attraction to the constellation even more significant!

"Why does she build Orion's belt only infrequently? Who knows? Dogs are not automated machines. Zeta creates when she is moved to!"

Dr. Raymond Blake, Canine Cultural Heritage Researcher:

"I wish I had a clear hypothesis to offer, as Ms. Winter's explanation seems to have traveled here from another planet. I do have to agree that the presence of stars appears to be the trigger for the dog's behavior; her infrequent performances may indicate that specific stars are important. Let us for a moment consider the Orion grouping. I looked at the dates

and the appropriate star maps and have to say that on each occasion of Zeta's performance Orion was either visible or would be later that evening.

"Despite that fact, the original trigger for this dog was the building of a campfire—and therein lies the clue to her motivation. To this breed of dog, campfires mean potential food, and it is possible that Zeta's behavior indicates hunger. Certainly the cross configuration she constructs from the eucalyptus bark could signify those first two sticks one puts down when building a fire. Her ancestors watched campfires being built almost every night, and this image would be imprinted in the psyche of the Australian Kelpie. Why Zeta doesn't engage in this behavior every night, I cannot say, other than that in the wild she would be unused to being fed on a daily basis, and so might only make her constructions when extremely hungry."

The Golden Retriever is firmly established as a gundog but its ancestors were in fact sheepdogs from the Caucasus in Russia. In 1868 a traveling showman brought a troupe of the Russian dogs to England, where they caught the imagination of a British lord. He purchased the troupe and in their new home in Scotland they were bred for the purpose of retrieving.

Life is a performance to Teddy, whose exuberant "Look at me!" approach to his world gives every indication of his Russian circus background. Born in a large litter of super-boisterous pups, he has developed into an adventuresome teenaged dog with an independent spirit. His curiosity knows no bounds. After our photographic session, he spotted a treacherous-looking rapid and decided to experience bodysurfing. Battered and gasping for breath, he regained his equilibrium and galloped off for a repeat performance!

Teddy
A Golden Retriever
. . . .

Teddy was introduced to us through a letter from his owner, which included a child's drawing of what appeared to be a hippopotamus peering out from behind a fortress of bright blue branches and toy dump trucks.

"My grandson, Luke, was given a squeaky rubber duck with a very realistic duck call. Teddy reacts to this duck in an extremely peculiar way. On hearing its squeak he at first looks anxious, then rushes about dragging articles into a kind of crescent shape. Luckily, Luke lost interest in his duck and we then confiscated it—poor Teddy was being run ragged with his building of crescent structures."

—Excerpt from owner's letter.

On further communication, we discovered that this dog built similar structures out of branches and sticks, particularly in the vicinity of rivers—but only when he heard a duck call.

We decide to photograph Teddy at sunrise during the duck-hunting season in the hope that natural duck calls would be present. Not a duck was in sight so we had to resort to using Luke's toy. Teddy shrank two inches, gathered himself together, and bounded across the river to a pile of wattle branches, which he then proceeded to carry across to an island of pebbles. Here he erected one of his infamous crescent sculptures and positioned himself between its protective arms.

Strangely, the only time the dog appeared anxious was at the precise moment of the duck call. Once he was in action, his joyful, exuberant nature returned.

Dr. Raymond Blake, Canine Cultural Heritage Researcher:
"This dog is obviously building duck blinds. His grandfather and numerous dogs in his genealogy have been used for duck shooting, which indicates that his genetic makeup is strongly geared toward retrieving ducks. The fact that he only builds these structures after hearing a duck call eliminates any other possible explanation for his behavior. As you can see, he crouches motionless behind his structures like a hunter waiting for ducks to respond to his call."

Penelope Winter, Animal Spiritualist and Telepathic Diviner:

"I am amazed that Dr. Blake can be so adamant in his theory. There are several factors that he is choosing to ignore completely. For instance, why does Teddy look so anxious on hearing the duck call? Why would he build crescent structures in the sitting room when there is no river, duck, or hunter in sight? I'm told that Teddy adores chasing ducks and does not race off to build a duck blind whenever he spots one.

"Interested in Teddy's nervous reaction to the duck call, I questioned his owner about his puppyhood. Teddy was the runt of a very large litter. He was teased unmercifully by his brothers and sisters and spent a lot of time hiding behind blankets, sweaters, and food bowls. By five weeks old he was pulling materials into a kind of protective structure. When he moved to his new home this rather timid personality faded, and he became the gleefully boisterous dog he is today.

"I don't think Teddy is aware of the connection between the duck call and duck shooting. It seems to me that the quack of the rubber toy reminds him of the shrill yaps of his bullying siblings and he is replaying his puppy response to this by building a protective cave or fortress whence he can do battle with his attackers."

Renegade is obsessed by rope. This all-consuming passion began when he was a small gangly puppy belonging to a mussel farmer and commercial fisherman. He was adopted by another family at eighteen months old, when his owner began taking longer trips to sea, but his love for rope has survived his change of lifestyle. He collects leashes, tapes, twine, and cords and is a menace at obedience competitions: his owner frequently finds numerous filched dog leashes carefully stowed under her car.

There must be a purpose to his rope thefts; he drags, drapes, and arranges them and feigns deafness if called away from his work. His owner has provided him with his own personal collection of ropes that he insists upon traveling with at all times.

Renegade
A German Shepherd
. . . .

Renegade was obviously in mussel-line mode on the evening we photographed him. It was as though he'd decided upon his design before selecting the black hairy ropes from his diverse collection and springing into action without any hesitation whatsoever.

Dr. Raymond Blake, Canine Cultural Heritage Researcher:
"Given the German Shepherds' background as tracking dogs, Renegade's affiliation with ropes is not surprising. He comes from a long-established line of working dogs, both in police work and Search and Rescue. A German Shepherd of this lineage would associate rope with the adrenaline rush of working in stressful situations and the subsequent reward when the job was complete. Several of this dog's ancestors have been involved in snow rescues in Europe and in New Zealand.

Climbers and skiers in avalanche country attach a long red cord to their belts in the hope that part of the cord would be visible if they were buried under the snow, alerting the rescue dogs to their position. In the less-distant past, this dog has a strong connection to the ropes used in mussel farming."

Penelope Winter, Animal Spiritualist and Telepathic Diviner: "Dr. Blake completely overlooks the most important message in Renegade's work: the distinct fish shapes he creates with his ropes. At a time when admitting to Christianity was extremely dangerous, early Christians used to draw a simple fish symbol in the sand with their feet to indicate their religious leanings. Also, fishing ropes were frequently arranged in that design by Christian fisherman. Renegade's previous owner was apparently a devout fundamentalist Christian, and Renegade began making his fish symbols during the difficult period of adjusting to his new owner. He very quickly bonded with Ani but his obsession with rope and fish symbols has continued."

Ochre appreciates the finer qualities of life. While she enjoys all the activities that are part of the business of being a dog, her favorite occupations are draping herself elegantly over soft furniture and, above all, picking flowers. Her owners are orchardists and have little time to give to the garden, so the flowers that do bloom are particularly precious. Ochre seems to agree, and tries to distribute the flowers more evenly around the garden. She picks off their heads with exquisite care and presents them to the orchard workers, visitors, and frequently to Skye, the other resident Vizsla. Skye is nonplussed and dips his head in either appreciation or embarrassment.

Two days after the death and burial ceremony of Ochre's friend Cora the German Pointer, three gleaming tulip heads were found lying on the gravesite. To this day no one has taken responsibility for their appearance. When interrogated, Ochre just gave an enigmatic grimace and wandered off to check on the roses.

Ochre
A Hungarian Vizsla
. . . .

Why would a Vizsla gather autumn leaves and mound them into separate piles of red and orange? Our dog, Ochre, has done this for the past two seasons and we cannot imagine what motivates her."

—Excerpt from owner's letter.

Ochre is a silken streak of copper with a gentle and slightly shy attitude. One moment she is a wiggling fun-loving dog showering affection upon all around her, and the next she is unreachable, focusing on movements in the distance or wind-carried sounds.

Research into the origin of the Vizsla is blurred by the mists of history, but there is little doubt that its ancestors accompanied the Magyar tribes that wandered the Russian steppes during the eighth century.

The Vizsla was considered a royal breed of the barons and warlords of Hungary and its aristocratic bearing seems to verify this lineage. These dogs were used as hunters, trackers, pointers, and retrievers of a wide variety of game. But nowhere in their background could we find reference to gatherers of autumn leaves.

Color appeared to be a vital component of Ochre's behavior. We attempted to photograph her at the end of summer before the trees turned orange. She was distinctly disinterested.

Four weeks later, Ochre had a completely different attitude toward leaves. At first she spent some time pointing and rummaging under fallen branches, then she turned her attention to the twigs of red and yellow leaves that we had snapped off the surrounding trees. Using techniques of carrying, scraping, kicking, and pushing she organized four piles in a line. After observing her work for a moment, Ochre collected several more branches and twigs laden with leaves and constructed a second line intercepting the first. Then she resumed foraging among the branches and chasing scents across the field.

Dr. Raymond Blake, Canine Cultural Heritage Researcher:

"I found this dog's behavior difficult to explain. The crucial factors

seemed to be season, color, and line formation. As I watched the dog observing the piles it suddenly occurred to me that the leaves as such were not important. They were symbolic of something in the dog's ancestral memory. Reds, browns, and oranges? Of course! The colors of pheasant feathers. If they were representing the game after a shoot, the piling and lining up made absolute sense.

"Traditionally, the pheasants were tied together in pairs and several of these were carried home by the gamekeeper and his assistants. However, after a particularly successful sporting day (or slaughter, depending on your point of view) the number of dead birds needing transportation could be astronomical. One method of solving this problem was to tie the birds to a long pole that two men could transport with ease. I believe that this dog was piling up her symbolic birds in readiness for tying them onto a pole; hence the two straight lines."

Penelope Winter, Animal Spiritualist and Telepathic Diviner:
"I can not see Ochre's design as two separate yet intercepting straight lines. It is very clearly the Christian symbol of the cross. The fact that she chose autumn leaves to build her cross is irrelevant; she used whatever was at hand. But like Dr. Blake I believe that the colors were important to her.

"The cross has a strong psychic energy and power and I could feel another influence as Ochre progressed to the second arm of the symbol. It was as though she were merely the vehicle through which a message was being revealed to us. I was picking up the words *Wiesseldorf* and *crusaders*, along with an uncomfortable sense of anguish and chaos. After discovering that Wiesseldorf is a Hungarian town, I researched the fortunes of the crusaders during their invasion of Hungary. Apparently in the year 1069 a troop of crusaders was massacred by the Hungarian army in retribution for their plundering of peasant villages and refusal to keep their promises. The slaughter was unexpected and violent, the very ingredients giving rise to lost souls trapped between the earth plane and the beyond. Perhaps the dog and I were being used to channel some kind of message from a tormented crusader's incarnate.

"The colors of yellow, orange, and red with glimmers of green gave the appearance of tarnished metal: copper, silver, and gold. Ignoring the fact that Ochre's work was built of leaves and viewing it peripherally, the design took on the form and color of a Christian cross or a discarded, bloodied sword."

The two Belgian Barge Dogs live with owner Julia, three horses, two cats, and a mob of sheep on a ten-acre farmlet adjoining an inlet. Jeda and Blakey are self-appointed Horse Welfare Officers and take their responsibilities very seriously. At least three times a day they toddle down the long drive to the horse paddock, check out the scene, and report back to their owner.

One particular evening, instead of their usual rough-and-tumble routine around the living room floor, the dogs appeared anxious and distressed. Blakey stationed himself by the back door while Jeda stared intently at Julia's face, clearly trying to communicate her unease. Unnerved by their strange behavior Julia opened the door and the bargies were off down the drive and into the paddock. Just visible in the cloudy moonlight was one of the horses lying alarmingly close to the fence. Her hind legs were entangled in the wire and she was unable to move.

"I still can't work out how the dogs knew," said Julia. "It's as though the dogs sensed the horse's distress by telepathy."

Jeda and Blakey
Belgian Barge Dogs
. . . .

Two small black box shapes with a spindly leg on each corner and large pricked ears catapulted down the wharf slipway to greet us: Blakey and Jeda, the Belgian Barge Dog double-act described by their owner as builders of driftwood triangles.

Jeda proved to be the more madly outgoing and industrious of the two; Blakey took a dim view of cameras and audience. The product of a chaotic childhood, Blakey, after being adopted by Julia at the age of three, presented a complex, enigmatic character vacillating between utmost joy and introspective withdrawal.

Julia, who lives in close proximity to a small slipway, noticed that the dogs occasionally snuck off to the wharf early in the morning. A fisherman alerted her to their mysterious activities: "Those dogs of yours. They do strange things down 'ere under the wharf. They make triangles out of

driftwood. Sometimes both of them do it and at others the male dog sits under the wharf and watches the female make these things. You should get them looked at, it's not normal."

The words "not normal" were music to our ears and we arranged to photograph Jeda and Blakey in action under the wharf at dawn.

Dr. Raymond Blake, Canine Cultural Heritage Researcher:

"The genetic heritage connections are obvious given the dogs' nautical history. Barge dogs, as their name suggests, were used as guard dogs on Flemish barges, and their vigorous, compact little bodies are ideal for scooting about boats and wharves. *Schipperkee*, their Flemish name, translates as 'Little Captain.'

"The triangles formed by sun-whitened driftwood represent the white wooden triangles strategically positioned to aid the maneuvering of

watercraft. The white triangle warns boats of the presence of underwater cables. One of the functions of the barge dog was to sit in the prow of the boat and bark at the triangles to alert the captain of their presence, particularly in foggy or dark conditions. While neither of these dogs has actually lived on a barge in his or her lifetime, their ancestors undoubtedly did. The image of these triangles will be indelibly imprinted on the genetic memory of this breed of dog."

According to Julia, the dogs began their triangle-building behavior after being taken for a ride on one of the fisherman's boats. The spot at which they landed and subsequently built their constructions does not display a cable-warning triangle.

Penelope Winter, Animal Spiritualist and Telepathic Diviner:

"I see a very powerful psychic connection happening here. The dogs' owner keeps a dream diary, and we discovered that the dogs only build their triangles on the mornings after their owner has had a vivid recurring dream depicting Native American tepees that rise up out of the desert and disappear as she approaches. She awakens with the residual visual memory of their white triangular shapes. The dogs, who sleep at the end of her bed, must be linking into her dream state; the white light emanating from the dreamtime images sends out vibrations that transfer to Blakey and Jeda. I've been aware of the possibility of this sort of transference, but this is the first time I've found proof that it occurs. This is *very* exciting, as it opens up all kinds of insights into thought transference."

Dr. Raymond Blake:

"While I acknowledge the coincidental nature of the dream connection, Ms. Winter's argument is obviously flawed. Teepees have no relevance to barge dogs. What possible motivation or telepathic communication could there be, given that the owner was not aware of the dogs' activity?"

Penelope Winter:

"Mr. Blake's comments indicate a lack of understanding of the nature of dogs and of thought transference. The dogs are caretakers of the dream. They aren't attempting to communicate with their owner; they are merely building a physical manifestation of the dream images they received."

McCoy and the Group
The Cuckoo of the Dogs
· · · · · · · · · · · · · · · · ·

McCoy is the cuckoo of the dog world. Whereas the cuckoo steals other birds' nests, McCoy lays claim to other dogs' inspirations and constructions. It is not clear whether McCoy does his cuckoo act because he lacks original ideas or because he disdains hard physical labor. We met this smart little Westhighland Terrier when photographing three Golden Retrievers renowned for their collaborative work with driftwood pyramids. McCoy has a rather serious disposition, or at least that is the image he presents to the world. Beneath his erect little body and sometimes-stern expression lurks a trickster with a subtle sense of humor.

McCoy took up referee position at a safe distance from the action and watched the Goldies' performance with a slightly supercilious air. Clifford, Teddy, and Andy were in their element, pausing only occasionally to catch their breath or to fight for possession of a particularly desirable piece of driftwood. Their goal: to erect another of their impressive cone-shaped sculptures. Teddy was obviously the supervising architect; he had come up with the original teepee sculpture that was the basis for the current design. Andy, Teddy's litter brother, caught on to the concept very

quickly, as is sometimes the way with siblings. One of his main concerns was to make it absolutely clear that Teddy was *not* in charge.

Clifford, a wise and serene older dog, was not interested in things hierarchical. Ignoring the boys' one-updogship, he got on with the business of building. Other dogs do not challenge Clifford. He quietly establishes his position on all matters and leaves the squabbling over minutiae to lesser beings.

At one point, McCoy, momentarily forgetting himself in the excitement, rushed in to supervise. Unfazed by his intrusion, the Goldies considered his intentions, then ignored his advice, and he soon resumed his position at the edge of the site. The little dog was obviously in a state of internal conflict. On one hand, he was trying to appear disdainful and largely disinterested. However, the quiver in his small wiry body and the surreptitious glances he threw at the retrievers' work gave the show away.

Once they completed the sculpture the Goldies wandered off, still jostling over a discarded stick. Quick as a flash, McCoy zoomed into action and, contributing a small twig as the pièce de résistance, claimed the sculpture as his own work, posing in front of it with obvious pride!

What will my dog do?

"But could Rover, my Labrador, build things like that?"

Throughout the research for this book we encountered many dog owners, a great many of whom were amazed at the constructions built by the dogs we photographed. They believed that *their* dog would not be capable of such compositions, but were nevertheless interested in ways of facilitating their dogs' creative abilities.

"Rover is completely clueless! He has never produced any kind of sculpture or design. He's only interested in food, fetching sticks, and barking at the cows in the neighbors' field."

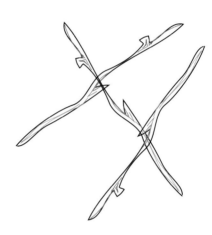

I pointed out to Rover's owner that her own young children, all producing vibrant and highly creative works of art, were given a wide variety of exciting materials to work with and an enormous amount of encouragement and positive feedback. Was Rover given the same kind of opportunities? She had to admit that it had never occurred to her to offer interesting objects to stimulate his creative juices.

Just as we would not expect a child who is deprived of crayons and paper to become a Picasso, so it is with dogs. On the other hand, not every dog provided with five wing bones, seven turkey feathers, and a set of deer antlers will necessarily produce a masterpiece. Obviously the dog works represented in this book are the most remarkable we encountered during our research. But many other dogs we met interacted with objects and materials at a less-sophisticated level.

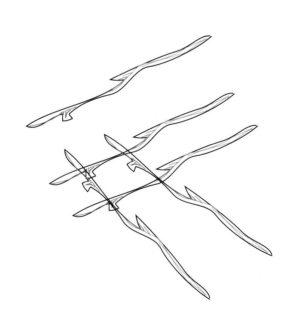

For Rover's owner, and all of us who share our lives with dogs; the first step in discovering our dogs' hidden talents is to observe their activities and to notice their choices. For example, next time you play "fetch" with your dog, instead of using the same stick each time, supply several and watch the pattern that emerges as your dog puts down each stick before racing off after the next. If she insists on using the same stick each time, mark the position on the ground where she drops it before you throw it again.

Give your pup a selection of objects and observe which ones he is attracted to and what he does with them. What will *your* dog do with a bag of feathers and a rock pool? Or give her a pile of sun-bleached bones—isolate two or three of them and watch her reaction. Try drawing lines in the sand and then offering the drawing tool to your dog.

Penelope Winter is convinced that telepathic communication occurs between dogs and their owners. Ever skeptical, I attempted this with my dog Tosca on the beach one afternoon. A stick lay in the sand about sixty feet away from where she stood. Focusing on Tosca, I willed her to walk over to the stick and pick it up. Success! I sent her the silent message to drop it into the sea, and again she complied. I now believe that if we can only reduce our internal chatter, this universal telepathic language to which dogs tune in with ease may also be available to us. Telepathy doesn't always work with such clarity, but it's certainly worth attempting and practicing, as it may enhance your relationship with your dog.

Dr. Blake's theory of inherited memory may also lead to a deeper understanding of your canine companion. Researching Rover's breed characteristics and, more importantly, his specific heritage may uncover fascinating clues to what makes Rover's behavior and personality unique. Try exposing him to the kinds of environments and materials that could trigger ancestral memories or links. Both Dr. Blake and Ms. Winter have avoided suggesting that dogs have an aesthetic sense. Many of the works in this book are aesthetically beautiful, and I am left with the uneasy feeling that we could be underestimating dogs' ability to make decisions based on some form of canine aesthetic awareness.

Perhaps animals inhabit powerfully imaginative inner territories that we humans, our minds so strongly governed by reason, have no access to? The challenge is to find the keys that will open these doors.

ACKNOWLEDGEMENTS

Planning, research, writing, and photography for this book have taken the better part of three years to complete. We are deeply indebted to the many people who have given so generously of their time and knowledge during this period.

Our special thanks go to the numerous dog owners who allowed us to observe and photograph their dogs at work. In particular we would like to mention Cynthia Tinsley, Paula Rowland, Sue McKee, Wayne Loader, Liz Brown, Bella Reid, Jim Black, Rachel Bewley and Paule Bowe, Caroline Roberts, Leslie Herrick, Liz Borland, Lindy Dalton, Ani Maddock, Jenny Burns, Lyndsay Doyle, Grant and Kay Jordon, Janette Barr, Adriane Boswell, Clive Randell, Julia Smith, Jane Sanders, Friar Milton, Nicki Scott, Mark Hight, Adriane Kent, and Rebecca Francois.

Most importantly we would like to acknowledge the dog builders without whom this book would have not been possible: Katya, Jessie, Towser, Jemima, Shadow, Luke, Dash, Minka, Emily, Abbie, Titch, Zeta, Teddy, Ochre, Jeda, Blakey, Kaysee, Andy, Renegade, Harry, Shylo, McCoy, Clifford, Tessie, Buck, and Flossie.

Through meeting these dogs and observing their works our attitudes and beliefs about dogs, particularly their intelligence, memories, and spiritual awareness, have been profoundly affected.

Penelope Winter and Dr. Raymond Blake opened our eyes to a wealth of possibilities in the sphere of dog behavior. While they both gave so generously of their time and expertise, they wish to avoid the loss of valuable research time by any publicity. Respecting their wishes, we agreed to protect their identities by altering their names in the writing of this book.

My thanks go to Melissa da Souza, my ever-patient guide, confidante, facilitator, and cocreator of *Dog Works*.

We give our heartfelt gratitude to the vets and all the staff at Massey University and Halifax Veterinary Center for their absolute dedication in trying to save Minka's life, and a special thank-you to Tracy for all those sleepless nights spent holding her paw.

SELECT BIBLIOGRAPHY

In addition to articles and books noted in the text, this list contains both titles of a general nature and more academic works for those who wish to read in detail about particular topics mentioned in this book.

Brown, B. *Dogs That Work for a Living*. New York: Funk & Wagnalls, 1970.

Burl, A. *Rings of Stone*. New York: Ticknor & Fields, 1980.

Castleden, R. *The Stonehenge People*. London: Routledge & Kegan Paul, 1987.

Chernak McElroy, S. *Animals as Teachers and Healers*. New York: Ballantine Books, 1996.

Coren, S. *The Intelligence of Dogs*. New York: Bantam Books, 1994.

Eysenck, H.J. and Sargent, C. *Explaining the Unexplained*. London: Weidenfeld & Nicolson, 1982.

Fogle, B. T*he Encyclopedia of the Dog*. Willowdale, Ontario: Dorling Kindersley, 1995.

Fowles, J. and B. Brukoff. *The Enigma of Stonehenge*. London: Jonathan Cape Ltd., 1980.

Herm, G. *The Celts*. London: Book Club Associates, 1976.

Marshall Thomas, E. *The Hidden Life of Dogs*. London: Weidenfeld & Nicolson, 1994.

Mondadori, A. ed. *The MacDonald Encyclopedia of Dogs*. London: MacDonald & Co., 1980.

Myers, A. *Communicating with Animals*. Lincolnwood, Ill.: Contemporary Books, 1997.

Richter, H. *DaDa: Art & Anti-Art*. Cologne, Germany: DuMont Schauberg, 1964.

Rowden, M. *The Talking Dogs*. London: Dorothy Meyer & Frau Heilmaier, 1978.

Sams, J. and D. Carson. *Medicine Cards*. Santa Fe: Bear & Co, 1988.

Sparks, J. The Discovery of Animal Behavior. Glasgow: Collins, 1982.

Stevenson, Dr. I. "Reincarnation." *Journal of Nervous and Mental Diseases*. Vol 1. (1976) pp 89 – 91.

Stubbs, D. *Prehistoric Art of Australia*. London: Macmillan Ltd., 1974.

Versluis, A. *Native American Traditions*. Shaftesbury, England: Element Books Ltd., 1994.

Walton, K. and R. Atkinson. *Of Dogs and Men*. Malvern Wells, England: Images, 1996.

Watson, L. *Lifetide*. London: Hodder and Stoughton, 1979.

Webster, R. *Omens, Oghams & Oracles*. London: Llewellyn Publications, 1995.

Wylder, J. *Psychic Pets*. Guilford, England: Biddles Ltd., 1978.

Yamazaki, T. and T. Kojimo. *Legacy of the Dog*. San Francisco: Chronicle Books, 1995.